Japanese Kimono Designs

Diane Victoria Horn

Stemmer House
PUBLISHERS, INC.
Owings Mills, Maryland

Introduction

THE KIMONO WAS THE TRADITIONAL DRESS of the Japanese people for nearly a thousand years, from the tenth century, when they broke with Chinese tradition, up to the Westernization of Japan during the late nineteenth century.

The word *kimono* means "a thing for wearing," and is a generic term used to describe three types of dress differentiated by the length and the width of the sleeve. Originally the *kosode* (small sleeve) evolved into the *hirosode* (wide sleeve) to the *furisode* (long swinging sleeve). Over a period of time the word "kimono" was used to describe each type of robe.

The basic kimono was a simply made garment with the T-shape formed from a single bolt of cloth. The materials used depended upon the season and on the occasion it was to be worn. For example, a *katabira* (summer kosode) might have been made of sheer hemp or ramie, a *yokui* (bathrobe) might have been made of cotton, and a theatrical robe could have been made of luxurious silk, satin, velvet or brocade. Whatever the material used, the kimono was full-length with an opening in the center front, and worn with the left side folded over the right. The two front panels were held in place by a sash *(obi)*. The woman's obi was four to five yards long, with the ends tied behind, in an intricate knot, over a small pillow. To hold the obi in place, a narrow silk cord *(obijimi)* was tied around the obi with the knot in front. The ends were weighted with pendants *(obidome)* of semi-precious stones or precious metals. The man's kimono was tied with an obi from which medicine boxes *(inro)* were suspended by a cord, with exquisitely carved toggles *(netsuke)* tied to the ends.

1

2

KIMONO DESIGNS

Though the kimono was a simply made garment, it gained novelty and distinction from the designs. Kimono design had its source in the refined and complex Japanese culture. Taste was rooted in the daily lives of the ruling classes, so that the cultural significance of kimonos was considerable. Many kimono designs were distinctly Chinese motifs, but the Japanese changed them to informally balanced, irregularly spaced and stylized naturalistic motifs or geometric patterns. Each design had a particular significance in Japanese life, with most elements drawn from the love of nature. Flowers of the Four Seasons, for example, were recurring motifs. The Peony that blossoms in spring symbolized nobility, wealth and honor. The Lotus blooms in the summer and was the symbol of purity and truth. Chrysanthemum, the flower that blossoms in the fall, represented longevity and strength, and the Plum Blossom, because it grows in the snow, symbolized nobility of character. Of all the seasons, autumn was the favorite of the Japanese, for the brilliant colors of the falling leaves were reminiscent of the end of nature's cycle, and a reminder of the transience of beauty and of human life.

Meandering vines were favorite plant motifs because the arabesques used by the artist formed a growth pattern and a visual logic of its own. Bamboo was also frequently used as a design motif and symbolized endurance and strength, with its ability to bend before the force of nature without breaking. Other designs frequently used on kimonos could be found on family crests (monsho). The design motifs used on crests were often inspired by nature.

Designs were made by dyers who kept catalogues (hiinakata) or fashion books of their individual creations, ready to present to customers. The dyer turned the white cloth into brilliant colors through batik, tie-dyeing and other creative processes. During early periods, basic decorating techniques were resist-dyeing (shibori) and embroidery. Woven decoration, however, producing palatial and courtly garments, was considered richer in quality. Resist decoration was used mainly to dye the clothing of the common people and was considered inappropriate for official occasions. In later times, resist dyeing achieved greater acceptance and was regarded as the basic decorating technique, in combination with embroidery and applied metallic leaf of silver and gold.

The colors of kimonos reflect the theme of the motif used in the designs. Since most of the designs were influenced by the love of nature, particularly flowers, the colors suggested the resplendent hues of grand gardens. The bounty of dyes derived from nature included red madder, purple cromwell, natural blue indigo, pink Japanese sunflower, aster, wisteria, iris, cherry, apricot and Japanese rose, as well as tints and shades from green leaves, brown bark, yellow-green plant roots, mauve bush cover and yellow, orange and red fruits.

Although all classes of people wore the kimono as a principal outer garment, the elaborately decorated robes, like those drawn in this book, were reserved for the court and attendants, and for special occasions. The man's kimono was usually simpler in design and more subdued in color, with the exception of those worn by male performers in the traditional Japanese theater.

The patronage of kimonos eventually passed from the military elite and warrior class (shogun) to the wealthy townsmen, who became the principle pa ons. This cultural shift was instrumental in the rapid spread of painted resist-dyeing (yūzen) and the production of fashion books. Some of the boldest patterns and colors date to the late seventeenth century, after the long prolific and creative period under the Tokugawa shoguns. Many designs were stimulated by the bold patterns of stripes and checks and vibrant colors of the popular *kabuki* costumes. These designs were considered vulgar by the samurai class, and in an attempt to alter the wave of extravagance, the shogunate passed laws that controlled what people wore. As a result, simpler patterns and more muted colors were worn by the common classes.

During the mid-nineteenth century, however, elegance was restored, with emphasis placed on softer colors and barely visible woven patterns. Embroidery and dyeing techniques were often restricted to the interior lining. The adoption of Western-style clothing in the early twentieth century reached such acceptance that the empress Teimei issued a decree that only kimonos would be worn at official and cermonial occasions, in order to restore the tradition.

At that time, young artists created a new style of kimono which was influenced by the Art Nouveau movement in Europe. Designs with motifs of curved lines, swirls and flowing water became very popular. Ironically, these re-imported designs had been painted by Japanese artists such as Hokusai in earlier centuries, and served as major inspiration for the Art Nouveau movement itself.

In the first half of the twentieth century, large industries, department stores and wholesale dealers began dealing with kimono producers. These organizations hired professional designers to produce quantities of kimonos with innovative designs. The twentieth-century designs on kimonos are extremely varied, responding to the various tastes of consumers around the world.

THE EVOLUTION OF JAPANESE HAIRSTYLES

   To make the dress complete as well as proper for the occasion, many accessories were worn with the kimono. In Japan, as in other cultures, hairstyles *(kamigata)* and dress closely parallel the course of social history. The changing fashions in Japanses hairstyles reflect the formation of an aristocratic class, the subsequent rise to power of the samurai, the rigid social stratification of the shoguns and the later modernization of Japan. Hairstyles also varied according to age and social rank. During the long period of peace under the Tokugawa shogunate, many varieties of new hairstyles for women appeared. Many styles were copied from men's styles, yet others were more artistic, with the hair being separated into five sections: forelocks, *"bin"* (right and left sidelocks), *"mage"* (bun) and *"tabo"* (rounded puffed-out bak hair). Much use was made of colorful hair ornaments, such as combs, to help keep the rolled or knotted hair in place. By the end of the nineteenth century, the hair iron was introduced from France, and waved hair became popular. By this time most young women wore their hair in Western styles, but middle-aged and older women tended to favor the traditional hairstyles. Today, traditional Japanese hairstyles, like kimonos, are seen only during special occasions.

Century: 10 11 12 13 14 15 16 17 18 19 20

3

   Another more functional kimono accessory was important to Japanese people when they disrobed. The *ikō* was essentially a crossbar on which kimonos were hung when not being worn. There were two types: those that stood on the floor *(ikō)* and those which were suspended *(tsuri-ikō)*. A variation of the ikō resembled a gate *(torii)*, and was made with two folding panels *(ikō-byō-bu)*. Wealthier households indulged in torii-styled kimono racks which stood an average of 5½ feet (166 centimeters) high, with crossbars spanning some 7 feet (210 centimeters), entirely finished in lacquer.

   Suspended racks were hung by robes or narrow notched boards attached to each end. The suspended racks were made in endless variety, from the most elaborate, of carved wood and treasured sheathed swords, down to the humblest, of plain lengths of bamboo.

Some other accessories worn with the kimono were the following:

ōgi, sensu	folding hand fan
uchiwa	round or oval nonfolding hand fan
geta	wooden clogs
hanten	a man's short coat worn by the working class
happi coat	worn by middle and lower classes of hte samurais
kamishimo	a man's formal outfit made up of a short-sleeved short coat worn over a kimono, and a skirt of the same material and color
sukiya	a small colorful handbag
tabi	footwear made of sturdy cloth fastened with metal clasps, with the big toe separated from the others; worn by workmen and also on formal occasions

THE KIMONO AS THEATRICAL COSTUME

Today, the kimono is still being worn in the traditional Japanese theaters. Heavy brocade and satin kimonos are worn as costumes with jackets, trousers, cloaks, fans, swords and masks worn as accessories. *Nō* (talent) robes are rich and colorful with bold designs made to create an impression on stage. The *kabuki* (singing and dancing) performer's costume is even more lavish. While both types of actors wear brilliant colors and designs, the kabuki performer wears elaborate stage make-up, while the Nō actor wears a mask.

The Nō mask completes the costume. The actor gives up his individuality when he puts on the carved wooden mask, and his interpretation of the part he plays is almost completely governed by the mask he has chosen. Each mask has its own individual position, which must be adhered to and brought to life by the actor's interpretation.

The actor's purpose in wearing luxurious kimonos on stage is to accomodate the expressive sweeps and gestures of the arms characteristic of the Nō drama. The drama begins with the mask, and the kimono is the visual flower which brings form to the flowering of the actor's talent.

a

b

c

d

5

Though the kimono is no longer the basic dress of Japan, it is still worn during the numerous *matsuri* (festivals) and ceremonies, and during theatrical performances. Collectors of art spend fortunes on antique kimonos. Unique two-paneled kimono screens, onto which fragile kimono fragments, as well as pages from kimono fashion books are pasted, can be found in numerous art collections. Painted folding screens and woodblock prints, with the kimono as the central design draped on racks, are also very popular interior-design elements.

Kimono designs have been a strong influence in the art world as well as in the fashion industry, and they have led to innovations and discoveries in the field of textiles. Kimono designs have inspired poetry, drama and music, and they are adapted by contemporary artists who use them in inventive ways.

In illustrating this book, each motif has been rendered either from an original kimono, a fragment, a kimono screen or a block print *(ukiyoe)*. The drawings are adaptations of the original designs rather than mechanical renderings, and can be utilized as decorative motifs on a variety of surfaces with limitless possibilities.

D.V.H.

This book is dedicated to my parents, Carrie and Lewis Horn, who have always been a constant source of encouragement and love in my life.

List of Illustrations

a

b

c

d

14

18

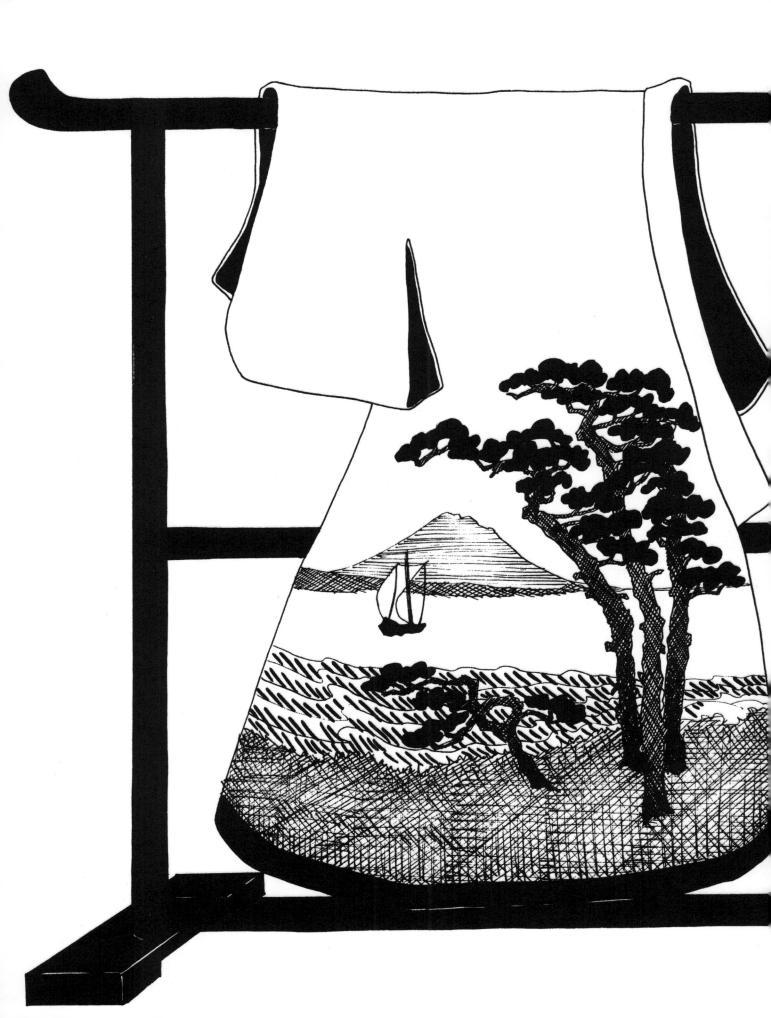

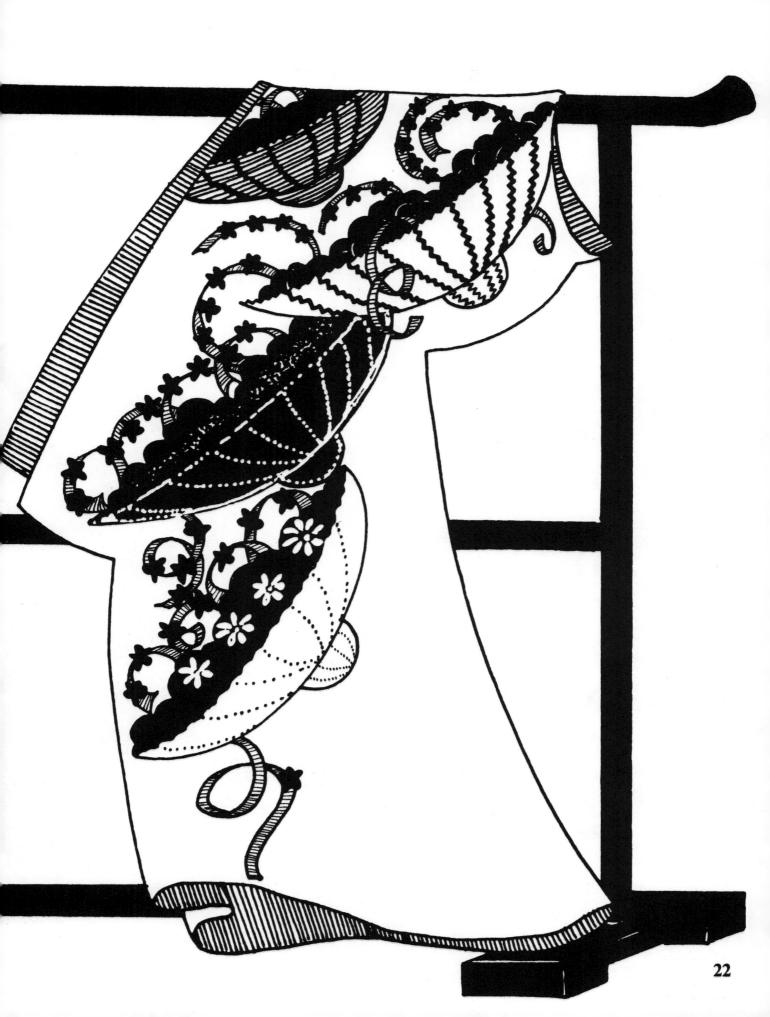

22

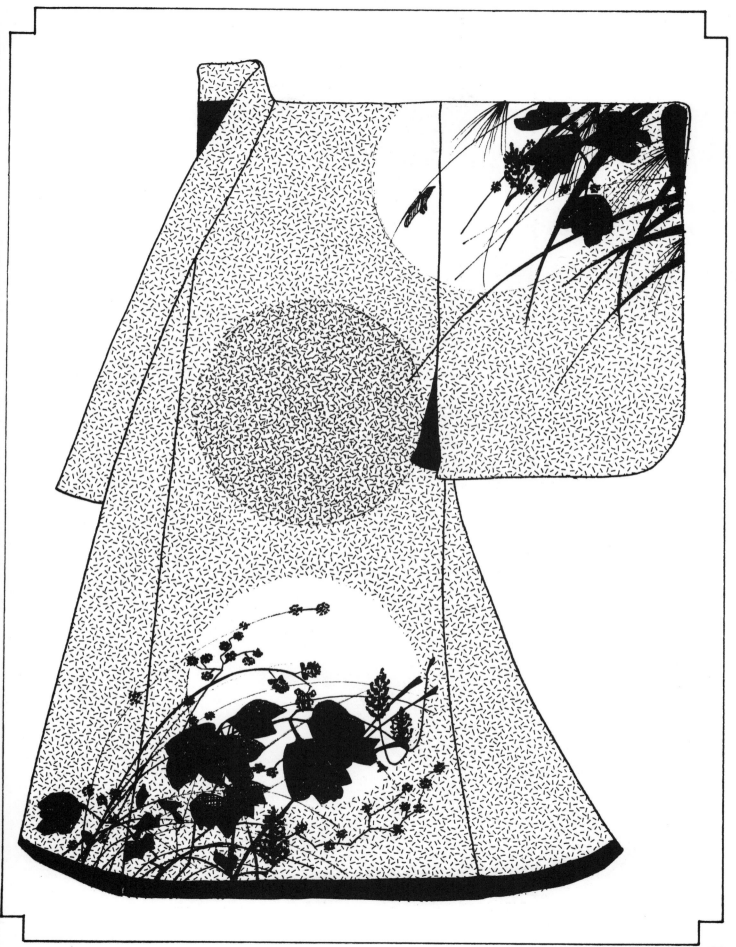

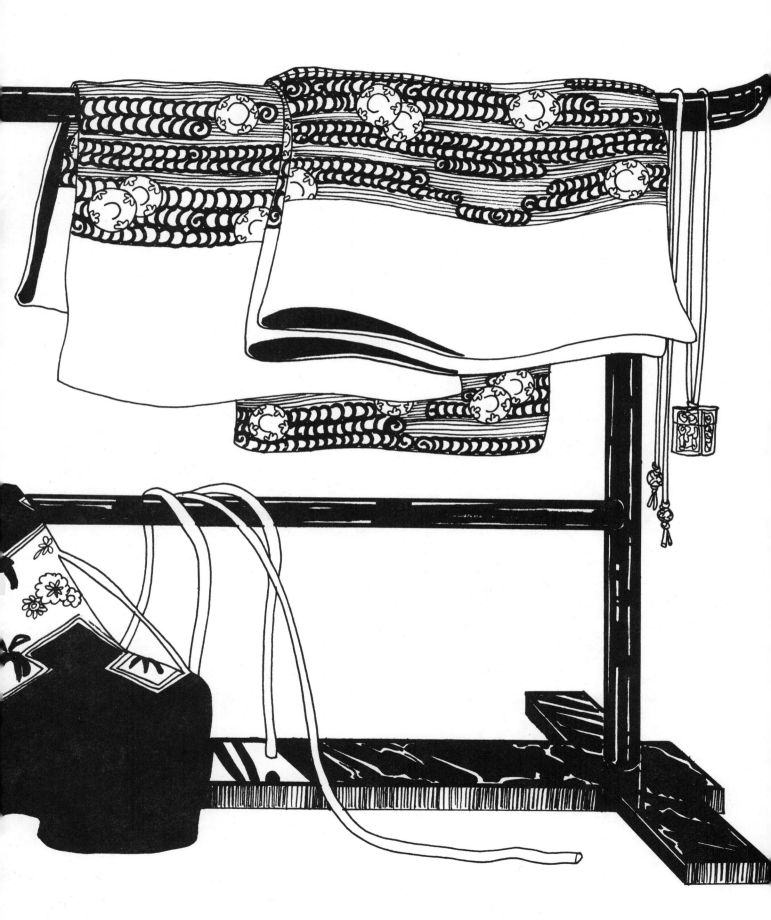

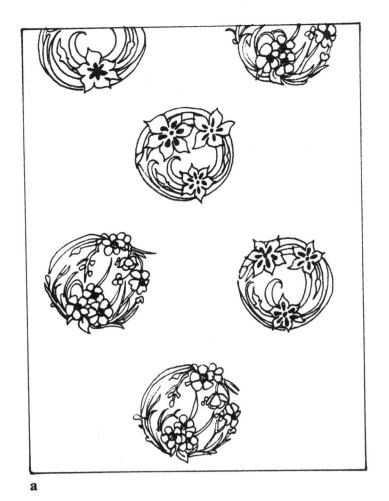

a

b

c

d

37

a

b

c

d

38

39

Designed by Barbara Holdridge
Composed in Times Roman by Brown Composition, Inc., Baltimore, Maryland
Printed on 75-pound Williamsburg Return Postcard and bound by
    United Graphics Incorporated, Mattoon, Illinois